JAPANESE ABC's

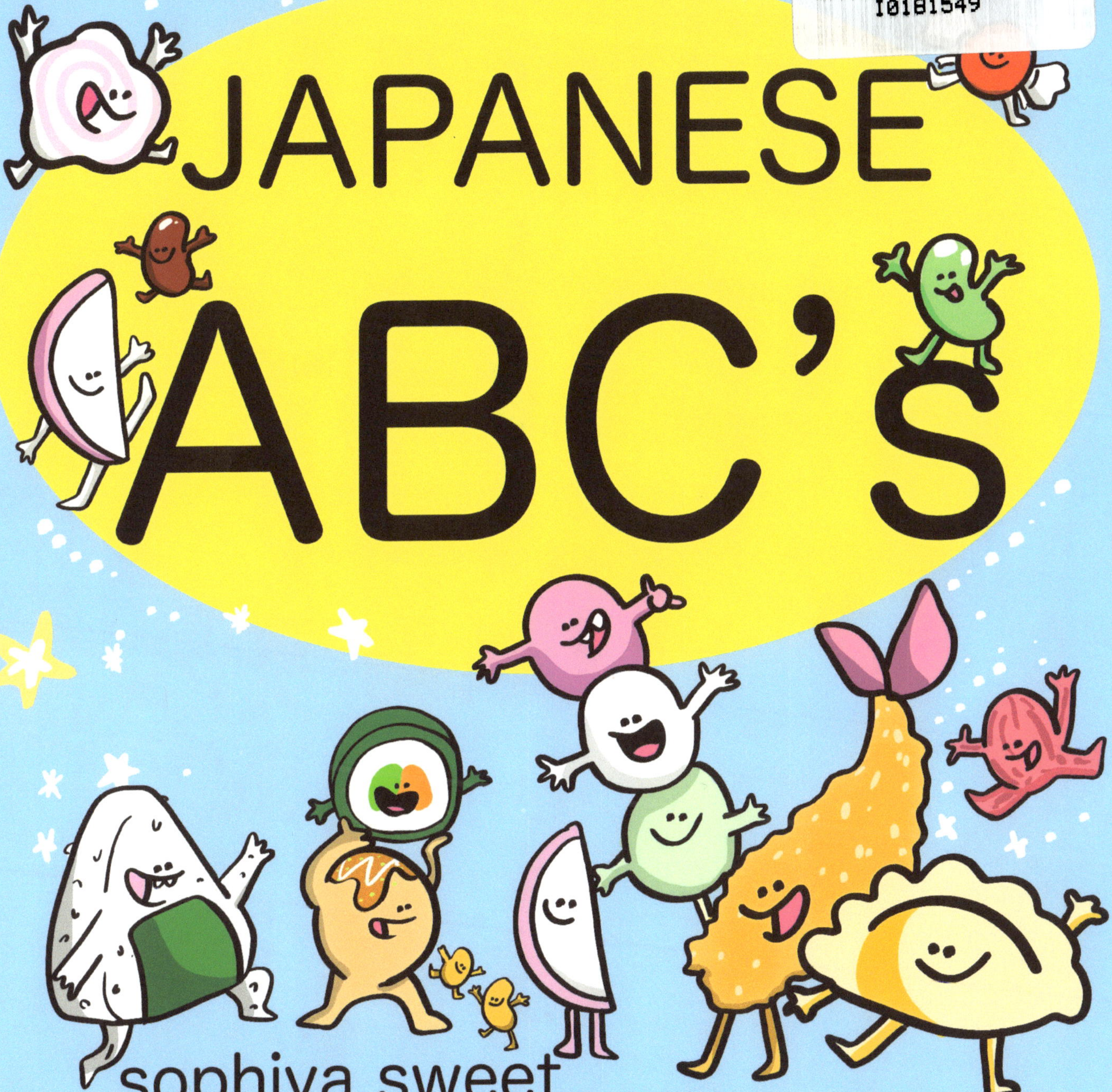

sophiya sweet

Japanese ABC's

Copyright © 2019 by Sophia Eberlein

All rights reserved. This book or any portion thereof may not be reproduced or used in any manner whatsoever without the express written permission of the publisher except for the use of brief quotations in a book review.

Copyright © Sophiya Sweet 2019 All Rights Reserved

Dedicated to Koji Ichida

Thank you Grandpa, for encouraging my love of art and writing!

いただきます!

I humbly receive!

Let's Eat!

Azuki

アズキ

Chankonabe

sumo's favorite!

ちゃんこ鍋

Dango

だんご

Edamame

えだまめ

Furikake

ふりかけ

Gyoza

ぎょうざ

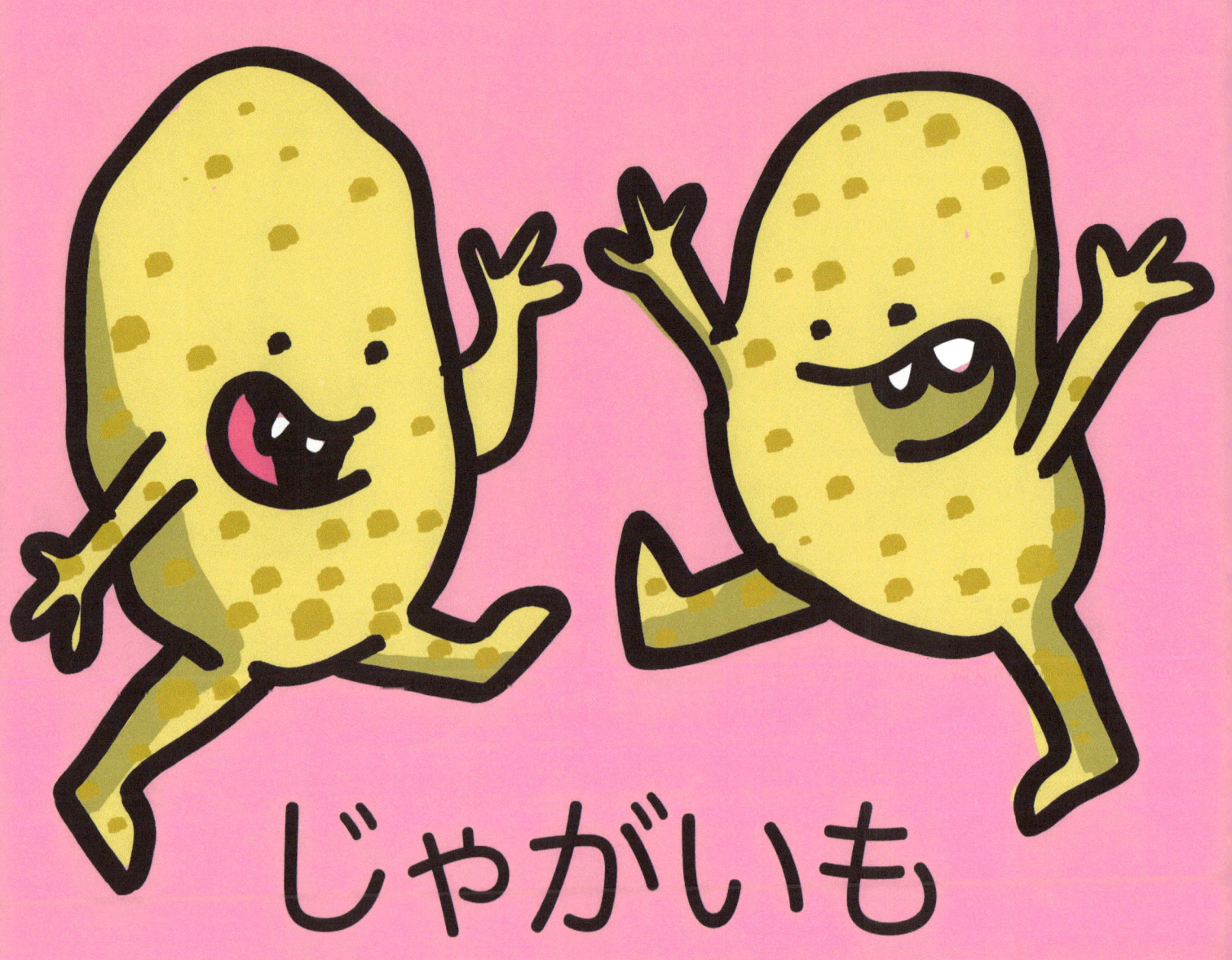

Kinoko

きのこ

Momo

もも

Natto

なっとう

Quirky Candy

おかし

Ramen

らーめん

Sushi

すし

Takoyaki

たこやき

Udon

うどん

Wasabi

わさび

eXtra rice

おおもり ごはん

Yuzu

ゆず

Zashiki

ざしき

ごちそう さま でした!

Thank you for the delicious meal!

About the Author

Sophiya Sweet is a Japanese American author from sunny Southern California!
She loves writing poetry, making music, and eating mochi!

When she's not munching on mochi, she enjoys illustrating children's books and learning to play different instruments!

Her first children's book "A Little World For You" is also available now on Amazon!

Sophiya Sweet's music is out now on Spotify, iTunes and Apple Music!

Weekly videos on her Youtube @SophiyaSweet

www.ingramcontent.com/pod-product-compliance
Lightning Source LLC
LaVergne TN
LVHW072058070426
835508LV00002B/160